Heaven is the End Game

A Fourteen-Day Meet Your Maker Challenge

Tamara Ann Valles

Tamara Ann Valles

WESTBOW
PRESS®
A DIVISION OF THOMAS NELSON
& ZONDERVAN

This book is a work of non-fiction. Unless otherwise noted, the author and the publisher make no explicit guarantees as to the accuracy of the information contained in this book and in some cases, names of people and places have been altered to protect their privacy.

WestBow Press books may be ordered through booksellers or by contacting:

WestBow Press
A Division of Thomas Nelson & Zondervan
1663 Liberty Drive
Bloomington, IN 47403
www.westbowpress.com
844-714-3454

Because of the dynamic nature of the Internet, any web addresses or links contained in this book may have changed since publication and may no longer be valid. The views expressed in this work are solely those of the author and do not necessarily reflect the views of the publisher, and the publisher hereby disclaims any responsibility for them.

Any people depicted in stock imagery provided by Getty Images are models, and such images are being used for illustrative purposes only.
Certain stock imagery © Getty Images.

Scripture quotations marked NIV are taken from The Holy Bible, New International Version®, NIV® Copyright © 1973, 1978, 1984, 2011 by Biblica, Inc.® Used by permission. All rights reserved worldwide.

Scripture quotations marked NLT are taken from the Holy Bible, New Living Translation, Copyright © 1996, 2004, 2015 by Tyndale House Foundation. Used by permission of Tyndale House Publishers, Inc., Carol Stream, Illinois 60188. All rights reserved.

ISBN: 978-1-6642-9444-8 (sc)
ISBN: 978-1-6642-9446-2 (hc)
ISBN: 978-1-6642-9445-5 (e)

Library of Congress Control Number: 2023904320

Printed in the United States of America.

WestBow Press rev. date: 08/09/2023

*To my friends and family who have been disillusioned by
circumstances, people, situations, losses, and all the things that make
up this crazy world we live in today. Heartbreak comes in different
ways. God can and will heal our hearts, because He loves us.*

To M.J. my inspiration "Savor every moment"

*To my friends who have helped to make this book possible
and have spirited me on, my cheerleaders, thank you!*

*To my husband who supports me and encourages
me in all things, thank you, and I love you!*

You all have blessed me and made this book a reality.

ACKNOWLEDGMENTS

I offer my gratitude and special thanks to the following:

- Kathy, Ginny, and Ralph for editing, proofreading, and typing this book and making it come to fruition

- Mike Miller for his free will insight

- my Ghost writer, the Holy Spirit

The invitation is open-ended. You pick the time and place. Today is as good a day as any to RSVP.

INTRODUCTION

To whom this may concern,

I'm just an ordinary person. If you know me, you know I'm not a genius, model, rich, or anything this world would call extraordinary. But God thinks you and I are special. I'm blessed with a wonderful husband, friends, family, a career I love, good health, etc. I've had trials and loss in my life like everyone, but I have always had my faith in God to lift me up.

My Lord is my Rock, Savior, confidant, comforter, friend, source of peace and joy, and so much more. He has taught me the true meaning of *love*.

Unconditional love means "no matter what."

Only my Creator can love me this way. My true Father in heaven. I want everyone to have the chance to feel the special love of a Father who loves you "no matter what." It's a love beyond human understanding.

God is love. It's that simple.

It's not my intent to convince, coerce, Bible thump, or make you feel uncomfortable. God put this in my heart and mind and put my pencil to the page to write an invitation directly to you. So you have an opportunity to meet him one-on-one.

Free will is a precious gift from God. It lets us love him with our "whole heart" because we want to, not because we have to.

This book began in my heart.

One day while talking to family members, I realized they were losing faith in God. Some friends were facing insurmountable trials and losses. Others had been believers in God, active in their churches, leaders, and very dedicated. They confessed to me that they just didn't believe in God anymore. Others just stopped going to church. Another had a terrible tragic loss and was so angry with God all they had left were anger and resentment. I know how God loves us. He doesn't want anyone to feel brokenhearted, empty, angry, or separated from Him. Why do these things happen to believers?

We have inherited "free will." Adam and Eve disobeyed God and ate the apple from the tree of knowledge. They were told by God not to, but they listened to Satan's lies and did it anyway. Just like Adam and Eve, we are God's children. Since that day in the garden, we were given free will, but we have given in to our desires. The world we live in is infected. It is cursed because Satan has full access to us. Our only protection is God. God gave us choice. He loves us that much.

Death for us is not the end. It's just the beginning.

I consider myself a prayer warrior when I see a need, or if I'm asked to pray for someone, I'm on it! My faith is strong, so I pray. I asked God specifically in prayer why some are taken from us so early. He showed me Isaiah 57:1 (NLT), a Bible scripture:

"Good people pass away; the godly often die before their time. But no one seems to care or wonder why. No one seems to understand that God is protecting them from the evil to come."

He is faithful. He answers my prayers in His own time. When I asked why my prayers aren't always answered concerning healing, He said, "Healing comes in all forms and when I call someone home to heaven, it is good."

So with a broken heart for my friends' and family's losses, I went before God and prayed for healing and a change of heart for the people I love. I kept praying and praying. I know God's promises, and He will answer in his time.

Then COVID hit!

Seeing the effects it had on our emotions, health, trust, and resolve, my prayers changed.

Revival:

to seek and to save

that which is lost.

The Bible has passages explaining a revival, an awakening in the souls of humans, and a renewed interest in coming to God. A lot of us believe we are living in the end times. Things that are written in the Bible are coming to pass; predictions are coming true. Among them, predictions of wars, weather changes, natural disasters, etc. The Bible says there will be a revival. So my prayers changed.

I asked God to bring on the revival. I prayed that people would turn to him in all the turmoil of our current times, including politics, war, COVID, death and despair. He gave me four words. "Revival starts with you!"

God was as clear as a bell! I was thinking, *Um, What? Wow! Really? Yikes!*

Then He showed me what that meant. So came the flood—the flood of words!

The knowledge that I was going to write a book! *Me! What?* I'm the woman who sits in the back of the church praising, singing, and praying. But don't get me too involved! I'm too busy! *Now the revival of the world is on me?*

So God started downloading ideas for the book. Not just a book, but a challenge! A chance to evolve, to understand, to open up to possibilities. An opening of the mind and soul to be able to enter a relationship with God. A way to commune with God. He can and will show you who He is and why things happen in our lives. He can comfort in ways humans cannot. He will listen and understand without judgment or shame.

This is your chance to see a future without the restraints of this life. To understand that everything has a purpose. The things you have survived and experienced in this life, God was with you. Because of the relationship Satan has with this world and our "free will," it is hard to see the truth.

Satan is the great deceiver, the author of lies, and a master counterfeiter.

Satan has been very good at blurring the line between right and wrong and good and evil. If you have been on this earth for a while, you see there has been a drastic shift in right and wrong. When you have a relationship with the one true God, you will be able to discern between the two, in real time, before you make the wrong choice. Without God to take our blinders off, we stumble through life numb and blind to our destructive tendencies. Without God, we live in a huge gray area of existence. no boundaries or rules. Everything is OK in moderation. *Really?* What a big fat lie from the devil!

If you have somehow received this book, I believe it is your destiny. It's in the grand design of your life. By reading it, it will change your life forever. If you finish the challenge until the end, it will give you a new perspective, understanding, and you will know another level of life. Also, it will give you hope for the future. It will answer questions, open discussions, and reveal truths. In the world we live in today, we all need hope.

Hope in one another, hope in world events, and hope in the future. The things that are unfolding on the world stage right now were predicted in biblical times. God has a plan for you. He has it under control. When you understand why these events are happening and what it means to you on a personal level, then you can see the big picture.

Many come to God as a last resort. Some call religion a crutch like it's a bad thing. The *New Oxford American Dictionary* describes religion as "a belief in and worship of a super human controlling power."

Yeah, that's not what I have with God; it is so much more. But you know what? Yes, I can and will call God my crutch. I can lean on Him anytime. He supports me. He holds me up when I am broken. He props me up and protects me as I heal.

I don't like to call myself "spiritual." There are too many examples of spirituality that don't include my God. I have a relationship with the one true God, and it's personal.

Relationship is the key. It's not enough to say you believe in God. The Devil believes in God! It's not enough!

I don't have to be perfect! *We* don't have to be perfect. Come as you are.

If perfection were the measurement, we would all be doomed to fail!

The objective is to have a one-on-one relationship with God.

Relationship is the key. It's not enough to say you believe in God.

The devil believes in God! It's not enough!

If I am hanging out with God in prayer and listening to what He wants of me, then I can rely on Him to guide my way. If I'm right with Him, I am right with myself. God loves me the way I am. If my relationship with Him is healthy, then I crave to spend time with Him and do His will and please Him, not the world.

I don't have to be codependent to this world and the people in it. It's not about being liked and fitting in. It's being true to my identity in Christ, about living true to how and why I was created and living my true purpose. When I stay on my path, my line of vision is farther and wider. I see the big picture more clearly. God has lifted the blinders off my eyes and has shown me more meaning to my life.

We all have a connection to God. When I have a strong connection, I have more hope for the future. I know, without a doubt, when I die, I will go to heaven. I will be engulfed in love, surrounded by peace. I will have no pain, no worries, and no anxiety about anything. Just pure joy, love, and peace. The residents of heaven, my friends and family, will be waiting with open arms, excited, overjoyed, and celebrating.

Heaven is the

ultimate healing

Heaven is my end game.

When we choose heaven as our end game, it means making a conscientious decision to seek God in all things. When we truly give ourselves over to the search for truth (concerning salvation and heaven), then we can open our hearts and minds to the possibilities. We can learn who God is and what He can do for us. Then you can understand heaven as your end game.

Sadly, heaven isn't for everyone. Yes, this is the truth. I've asked people to describe their ideas of heaven and hell. Some people say, "Everyone goes to heaven." No, that's a lie from the devil. Others say there is no hell. Another lie! Some say there is no God. Big-time whopper lie! I've heard heaven is on earth, hell is on earth, or hell is where the fun people go! Please believe me: hell isn't fun! Why do you think they call it hell? More lies!

The path is narrow.
There are obstacles,
but when it gets
dark, we have a light
to guide our way.

If you choose to take this challenge, you will get an introduction to the real, one and only three-in-one God who saves. It is a road map that paves the way to heaven.

If you allow yourself to finish this fourteen-day challenge, it will change your life. We all have free will to choose our paths. One way or another, your life will change, forever, because you will know the Truth. You will have met your Maker.

If you commit yourself to God, you are guaranteed a place at the table in heaven. Eternity is forever!

Make heaven your end game!

Heaven could be for everyone if everyone wanted to go. Life is a serious game. Let Jesus be your coach.

FOURTEEN-DAY "MEET YOUR MAKER" CHALLENGE

This challenge is an opportunity to find hope, peace, love, acceptance, and direction in a broken world.

It's a simple way to come to God, no matter your circumstances, and to find purpose in your life.

This is not

- a cult

- a pyramid scheme

- an organized religious institute

- a specific church.

It is

- a way to find God on your terms

- a chance to introduce yourself to your Creator

- a road map to begin a journey

- a method to have an individual, one-on-one relationship with God

- an opportunity to start trusting in the one who loves you unconditionally

- a means to understand who you are according to the one who made you.

Nothing can fill the void in your heart reserved for God. He is the missing piece to the puzzle.

Humans are created in the image of God (James 3:9).

There is a place reserved in our hearts for God to reside.

This challenge can fill that void, the space in your heart reserved only for God.

We as humans try to fill the void with a lot of things: people, food, drugs, money, sex, possessions, relationships, gaming, status, etc.

It's never enough.

When we fill the void with God, we can finally find peace and love. We all have a longing to find love and to be loved. Human love is never enough to fill the void. Without God, we continue to yearn for something more. We try to put all kinds of things in this place in our hearts, but nothing seems to fit. It's the wrong piece to the puzzle.

Your journey has led you here. Be fearless and open the door.

Please try this Fourteen-day "Meet Your Maker" Challenge.

You may feel

- that God let you down

- you have had a church experience that didn't feel real or complete

- like people in the church let you down

- that parents, friends, etc. let you down

- disappointed in Christian television personalities

- incomplete

- like something is missing

All you need is to

- be open to the possibility of God

- come as you are

It's that simple!

Matthew 17:20 (NIV) says, "Truly I tell you, if you have faith as small as a mustard seed, you can say to this mountain, 'Move from here to there,' and it will move. Nothing will be impossible for you."

FOURTEEN-DAY "MEET YOUR MAKER" CHALLENGE

If you knock,
the door will be opened.

If you seek,
you will find.

I invite you to take this simple challenge to meet my God.

He is amazing!

Have a little faith
as small as a mustard seed.

Watch it grow
just a few minutes
a day.

Love,
Tammy

Question God

and wait. He will

answer in His time.

When the challenge starts, you will have a concept to ponder, a prayer to recite, and scriptures from the Bible to support the message.

Then shut your eyes for at least three minutes and think about the message.

Don't be surprised if God quietly speaks to your mind.

Open yourself up to commune with him after each day of the challenge.

After your meditation on the message, journal and answer the questions. It's an important part to see your progress and journey.

God is waiting with open arms.

DAY 1:
LET'S BEGIN!

CONCEPT

Come as you are, no matter who you are,
no matter what you've done.

PRAYER

*God, I am willing to accept
the possibility that You exist.*

Surrender to

the possibilities.

Matthew 7:7–8 (TLB)

Ask and you will be given what you ask for. Seek and you will find. Knock, and the door will be opened.

For everyone who asks, receives. Anyone who seeks finds. If only you will knock, the door will open.

James 4:8 (ERV)

Come near to God, and he will come near to you.

Hebrews 11:6 (AMP)

But without faith it is impossible to walk with God, and for whoever comes near to God must believe that God exists and that he rewards those who earnestly and diligently seek him.

For three minutes, sit still, shut your eyes,
and see what the Lord has for you today.

Unconditional love

means just that.

Journal

How do you feel? _____

_____

_____

_____

_____

_____

What, if anything, did God show you? _____

_____

_____

_____

_____

_____

How could this change your life? _____

_____

_____

_____

_____

_____

_____

Look around
and see the beauty
of His creation.

DAY 2

CONCEPT

I am worthy of unconditional love.

PRAYER

God, if You exist, show me. Let me experience
the world around me through Your eyes.

The beauty to come

is so much more.

Luke 10:23 (NLT)

Jesus said to His disciples, "Blessed are the eyes that see what you see. For many prophets and kings longed to see what you see, but they didn't see it, they longed to hear what you hear, but they didn't hear it."

Psalm 34:8 (NKJV)

Oh, taste and see that the Lord is good. Blessed is the man that trusts in him.

Psalm 119:18 (TLB)

Open my eyes to see wonderful things from your word.

Romans 8:37–39 (TLB)

But despite all this, overwhelming victory is ours through Christ who loved us enough to die for us. For I am convinced that nothing can ever separate us from his love. Death can't, and life can't. The angels won't, and all the power of hell itself cannot keep God's love away. Our fears for today, our worries about tomorrow, or where we are—high above the sky, or in the deepest ocean—nothing will ever be able to separate us from the love of God demonstrated by our Lord Jesus Christ when he died for us.

For three minutes, sit still, shut your eyes,
and see what the Lord has for you today.

Love each other just

as God loves you.

Journal

How have you felt love in your life? _____

_____

_____

_____

_____

_____

God's love comes in blessings. Can you list the blessings in your life?

_____

_____

_____

_____

_____

_____

_____

_____

_____

_____

_____

_____

_____

Happiness can

become a habit.

DAY 3

CONCEPT

Misery loves company.

PRAYER

God, I deserve to be happy. Please show me
joy. Help me reject any negative thought.

When mayhem surrounds you, keep your eyes lifted up to the heavens.

Psalm 30:11–12 (TLB)

Then he turned my sorrow into joy! He took away my clothes of mourning and clothed me with joy, so that I might sing glad praises to the Lord instead of lying in silence in the grave. O Lord my God, I will keep on thanking you forever!

Philippians 4:4–7 (TLB)

Always be full of joy in the Lord; I say it again, rejoice! Let everyone see that you are unselfish and considerate in all you do. Remember that the Lord is coming soon. Don't worry about anything; instead, pray about everything; tell God your needs, and don't forget to thank him for his answers. If you do this, you will experience God's peace, which is far more wonderful than the human mind can understand. His peace will keep your thoughts and your hearts quiet and at rest as you trust in Christ Jesus.

Romans 15:13 (ESV)

May the God of hope fill you with all joy and peace in believing, so that by the power of the Holy Spirit you may abound in hope.

Psalm 94:19 (TLB)

Lord, when doubts fill my mind, when my heart is in turmoil, quiet me and give me renewed hope and cheer.

For three minutes, sit still, shut your eyes,
and see what the Lord has for you today.

Negative thoughts are a cancer. They will kill your joy.

Journal

List any negative thoughts, including resentments. Give them to Jesus forever. Set yourself free. _____

_____

_____

_____

_____

_____

_____

How do you feel? If you still feel emotional attachments, ask Jesus to take them to the cross *forever*. Do this daily with negative emotions and resentments.

_____

_____

_____

_____

_____

_____

_____

_____

_____

_____

_____

God surrounds you.

He is everywhere, always.

DAY 4:
KEEP GOING!

CONCEPT

You are not alone.

PRAYER

*God, show me that a true
relationship with You is possible.*

As your faith grows,
you will gain strength
in the Lord.

1 Chronicles 16:11 (ESV)

Seek the LORD, yes, seek his strength and seek his face continually.

Matthew 28:20 (TLB)

And be sure of this—that I am with you always, even to the end of the world.

Psalm 27:10 (TLB)

Even if my father and mother abandon me, the LORD will hold me close.

Joshua 1:9 (TLB)

Yes, be bold and strong! Banish fear and doubt! For remember the LORD your God is with you wherever you go.

For three minutes, sit still, shut your eyes,
and see what the Lord has for you today.

Nothing can come

against you and

defeat you with God

in your corner.

Journal

The Lord is with you. What does His presence feel like? _____

_____

_____

_____

_____

_____

_____

If you have a personal relationship with God, how would you like it to change your life? _____

_____

_____

_____

_____

_____

_____

_____

_____

_____

_____

_____

_____

_____

Love has many counterfeit names: lust, infatuation, sex, etc. God's love is pure and unconditional.

DAY 5

CONCEPT

Human relationships are not enough
to fill the void in my heart.

PRAYER

*God, let me feel the difference between human love and
Your pure, divine love that is unconditional.*

His love for us has

no boundaries.

1 John 4:16 (ESV)

So, we have come to know and believe the love that God has for us. God is love, and whoever abides in love abides in God, and God abides in him.

Psalm 136:26 (ESV)

Give thanks to the God of heaven, for his steadfast love endures forever.

1 John 4:19 (ESV)

We love, because he loved us first.

1 John 4:8 (ESV)

Anyone who does not love does not know God, because God is love.

1 John 3:1 (NIV)

See what great love the Father has lavished on us, that we should be called children of God! And that is what we are! The reason the world does not know us is that it did not know him.

John 15:13 (NIV)

Greater love has no one than this, to lay down one's life for his friends.

For three minutes, sit still, shut your eyes,
and see what the Lord has for you today.

Past relationships are part of the journey to finding God's love.

Journal

Have you ever had relationships that were not healthy? You can ask Jesus to heal you of the past and help you to make better choices in the future.

_____

_____

_____

_____

_____

Write down their names as you hand them to Jesus. Cross them off your list forever.

_____

_____

_____

How could having God love you unconditionally change the way you see yourself? _____

_____

_____

_____

_____

_____

_____

God can take away the

unhealthy appetites

and replace them with

cravings for joy.

DAY 6

CONCEPT

The forces and desires of this world
do not promote true happiness.

PRAYER

*God, please stop me from trying to fill my void with addictions,
distractions, and/or obsessions and possessions.*

Money is not the
root of all evil; it is
the love of money.

1 Corinthians 10:13 (TLB)

But remember this—the wrong desires that come into your life aren't anything new or different. Many others have faced exactly the same problems before you. And no temptation is irresistible. You can trust God to keep the temptation from becoming so strong that you can't stand up against it, for he has promised this and will do what he says. He will show you how to escape temptation's power, so that you can bear up patiently against it.

1 John 2:16 (TLB)

For all these worldly things, these evil desires—the craze for sex, the ambition to buy everything that appeals to you, and the pride that comes from wealth and importance—these things are not from God. They are from this evil world itself.

Hebrews 13:5 (TLB)

Stay away from the love of money; be satisfied with what you have. For God has said, I will never, never fail you nor forsake you.

For three minutes, sit still, shut your eyes,
and see what the Lord has for you today.

*Don't place anything
in life with a higher
value than God.*

Journal

What things do I need to change in my life to gain true happiness? _____

_____

_____

_____

_____

_____

What is God showing me? _____

_____

_____

_____

_____

_____

What things do I use to fill my void? List them, and give them to Jesus. ___

_____

_____

_____

_____

_____

_____

When you weep, God weeps with you. He feels your pain.

DAY 7:
HALFWAY THERE!

CONCEPT

Life is not perfect or without trials, heartache, and loss.
God sent His own Son, Jesus, to live here
on earth to experience human suffering, loss, and finally death
on the cross. He understands your life.

PRAYER

*Lord, please be my help in times of need. Thank You for understanding
and seeing my personal struggles. Thank You for living a human life.*

Trust that God will

keep your boat afloat.

Hebrews 13:6 (TLB)

That is why we can say without doubt or fear, "The Lord is my Helper, and I am not afraid of anything that mere man can do to me."

1 Peter 5:6–7 (TLB)

If you humble yourselves under the mighty hand of God, in his good time he will lift you up. Let him have all of your worries and cares, for he is always thinking about you and watching everything that concerns you.

Proverbs 3:5–6 (ESV)

Trust in the Lord with all your heart, and do not lean on your own understanding. In all your ways acknowledge him, and he will make straight your paths.

Isaiah 43:2 (TLB)

When you go through deep waters and great trouble, I will be with you. When you go through rivers of difficulty, you will not drown! When you walk through the fire of oppression, you will not be burned up—the flames will not consume you.

For three minutes, sit still, shut your eyes,
and see what the Lord has for you today.

An all-knowing God knows you inside and out.

Journal

Do you feel the comfort of God's presence? How does it feel to know God has your back, in every aspect of your life? _____

_____

_____

_____

_____

_____

Ask God to show you specifically how He has helped you in your life. List the ways below. _____

_____

_____

_____

_____

_____

_____

_____

_____

_____

_____

_____

He is omnipresent—

always and forever.

DAY 8

CONCEPT

If you are everywhere, let me feel Your presence.

PRAYER

*Show me signs that You are with
me always—to guide and comfort me.*

Pray for protection, and

He will send His angels

to watch over you.

Isaiah 41:10 (TLB)

Fear not, for I am with you. Do not be dismayed. I am your God. I will strengthen you; I will help you; I will uphold you with my righteous right hand.

Joshua 1:9 (TLB)

Yes, be bold and strong! Banish fear and doubt! For remember, the Lord your God is with you wherever you go.

Deuteronomy 31:8 (TLB)

Don't be afraid, for the Lord will go before you and will be with you; he will not fail or forsake you. Do not be afraid; do not be discouraged.

Psalm 23:4 (TLB)

Even as I walk through the dark valley of death, I will not be afraid, for you are close beside me; guarding, guiding all the way.

Zephaniah 3:17 (ESV)

The Lord your God is in your midst, a mighty one who will save; he will rejoice over you with gladness; he will quiet you by his love; he will exult over you with loud singing.

For three minutes, sit still, shut your eyes,
and see what the Lord has for you today.

Jesus is an amazing Counselor. Share your life with Him.

Journal

How does it feel to know that God is everywhere, omnipresent? _____

_____

_____

_____

_____

_____

List signs how God has guided you or comforted you recently. _____

_____

_____

_____

_____

_____

_____

_____

_____

_____

_____

_____

_____

_____

When your burdens are heavy, let Jesus carry the load.

DAY 9

CONCEPT

Come to me if you are weary and burdened,
and I will give you rest.

PRAYER

Please take away my cares
and worries and give me peace.

All things work

together for good for

those who trust and

are called to Him.

Psalm 55:22 (AMPC)

Cast your burden on the Lord, and he will sustain you; he will never permit the righteous to be moved.

Romans 15:13 (ESV)

May the God of hope fill you with all joy and peace in believing, so that by the power of the Holy Spirit you may abound in hope.

John 14:27 (ESV)

Peace I leave with you; my peace I give to you. Not as the world gives do I give to you. Let not your hearts be troubled, neither let them be afraid.

Psalm 86:15 (ESV)

But you, O Lord, are a God merciful and gracious, slow to anger, and abounding in steadfast love and faithfulness.

Romans 8:28 (ESV)

And we know that for those who love God all things work together for good, for those who are called according to his purpose.

*For three minutes, sit still, shut your eyes,
and see what the Lord has for you today.*

Travel light. Let Jesus carry your bags.

Journal

Today lay your burdens down at Jesus's feet. Write them down and give them to Jesus. _____

_____

_____

_____

_____

_____

How does that make you feel to unload the cares and worries of this life?

_____

_____

_____

_____

_____

_____

_____

_____

_____

_____

_____

_____

_____

Exercise your faith.

Test the water.

DAY 10:
THIS PART IS GOOD!

CONCEPT

Your Creator is three in one.

Father—Creator.

Son—Savior, mentor, friend, confidant,
counselor, and so much more!

Holy Spirit—A direct line to the Father and Son, the whisper
you hear, your conscience, your guide to a righteous life.

PRAYER

Help me to meet and understand
the power of the Trinity (three in one).

The complexities of God

are astounding, not

unlike the human brain.

Matthew 28:19 (ERV)

So, go and make followers of all people in the world. Baptize them in the name of the Father and the Son and the Holy Spirit.

John 1:14 (ERV)

The Word became a man and lived among us. We saw his divine greatness—the greatness that belongs to the only Son of the Father. The Word was full of grace and truth.

John 14:16–17 (TLB)

If you love me, obey me; and I will ask the Father and he will give you another Comforter, and he will never leave you. He is the Holy Spirit who leads into all truth. The world at large cannot receive him, for it isn't looking for him and doesn't recognize him. But you do, for he lives with you now and someday shall be in you.

John 14:6 (TLB)

Jesus told him, "I am the way—yes, and the Truth and the Life. No one can get to the Father except by means of me."

For three minutes, sit still, shut your eyes,
and see what the Lord has for you today.

God is complex and complete: Father, Son, and Holy Spirit.

Journal

What is God saying to you today? Are you feeling God's presence?

_____

_____

_____

_____

_____

_____

If you have questions, ask God and list your questions—then the answers when received.

_____

_____

_____

_____

_____

_____

_____

_____

_____

_____

_____

_____

We are all sinners.

Not one of us is perfect.

DAY 11

CONCEPT

The definition of sin: "anything that separates you from God."

Good news! Sin is easily forgiven.
Stop doing it and ask Jesus for forgiveness.

PRAYER

Jesus, please forgive me for my sins.
I do not want to be separated from You. Now that I am forgiven,
help me to stop doing the things that keep me from You.

We are all works in progress, never perfect but striving to be better.

Romans 6:23 (ESV)

For the wages of sin is death, but the free gift of God is eternal life in Christ Jesus our Lord.

1 John 1:9 (ESV)

If we confess our sins, he is faithful and just to forgive us our sins and to cleanse us from unrighteousness.

Ephesians 2:4–5 (ESV)

But God, being rich in mercy, because of the great love with which he loved us, even when we were dead in our sin, made us alive together with Christ—by grace you have been saved.

For three minutes, sit still, shut your eyes,
and see what the Lord has for you today.

Ask to be forgiven.

Forgiveness is

for the asking.

Journal

Sins are forgiven daily. List the things that make you stumble. _____

_____

_____

_____

_____

_____

_____

Ask Jesus to set you free from repeating the same sin over and over. How does this make you feel, to be free from this sin? _____

_____

_____

_____

_____

_____

_____

_____

_____

_____

Not one person is better than another. We are all the same, waiting for forgiveness.

DAY 12:
THIS IS GREAT!

CONCEPT

Every day is a battle for your soul. The devil wants you,
but God wants you more. Satan is the author of lies, confusion,
and deception. He tries to lure you with empty promises that
lead you away from God. If it feels wrong, it probably is wrong.
The Holy Spirit whispers and speaks to your heart and mind.
He will guide you. Listen to the Spirit of God.

PRAYER

*Lord, please help me to see the truth and show me what God deems
to be harmful to me. Help me to see when Satan is trying to draw
me in. Place heavenly protection around me. Help me to hear and
feel the Holy Spirit's guidance and to clearly see what is true.*

Ask God for protection and to see the truth. Don't let the devil fool you with his imitations and sleight of hand.

1 Corinthians 10:13 (ISV)

No temptation has overtaken you that is unusual for human beings. But God is faithful, and he will not allow you to be tempted beyond your strength. Instead, along with the temptation he will also provide a way out, so that you may be able to endure it.

2 Thessalonians 3:3 (ESV)

But the Lord is faithful. He will strengthen you and protect you against the evil one.

Ephesians 4:27 (TLB)

For when you are angry, you give a mighty foothold to the devil.

1 Timothy 4:1 (TLB)

But the Holy Spirit tells us clearly that in the last times some in the church will turn away from Christ and become eager followers of teachers with devil-inspired ideas.

For three minutes, sit still, shut your eyes,
and see what the Lord has for you today.

The devil attacks

by sowing seeds of

doubt. Don't give

him fertile ground.

Journal

Tell Satan he has no power over you, through Christ Jesus. _____

_____

_____

_____

_____

_____

In what ways have you experienced the devil messing with you? Negative thoughts? Fear? Despair? You will never... You're not good enough... _____

_____

_____

_____

_____

_____

Can you list some devil-inspired ideas you have noticed lately? Hand them over to Jesus. Ask Jesus to destroy them forever. _____

_____

_____

_____

_____

Jump out and free-fall. Let Jesus be your parachute.

DAY 13:
ALMOST FINISHED!

CONCEPT

God did not create robots. He gave us free will to run our lives daily. We are not designed to go it alone. Trust God to take over every day. Trust in Him. Our will is what makes us vulnerable to bad decisions and rebellion.

To "let go and let God" gives a peace beyond understanding. He knows everything about you. He knows your daily struggles and will always be here for you. Put God first in your life. Before your spouse, parents, kids, and work. Have faith that God is in control.

Let Jesus be the driver. Take your hands off the wheel.

PRAYER

Lord, help me to give over my free will to You today and every day. Let Your will be done. Help me to believe You have a perfect plan for me. You will be with me always to guide me through every day and every aspect of my life. Help me to understand the depths of Your love and have faith that You are in control. Because all that happens to us is working for our good if we love God and are fitting into His plans for us.

My will: frustrating results

His will: peace

The things of this world will pass away, but hope is eternal. Our hope is in Jesus Christ.

John 16:33 (ESV)

I have said these things to you so that in me you may have peace. In the world you will have tribulation. But take heart; I have overcome the world.

Philippians 4:19 (ESV)

And my God will supply every need of yours according to his riches in glory in Christ Jesus.

Joshua 24:15 (CEV)

But if you don't want to worship the Lord, then choose here and now! Will you worship the same idols your ancestors did? Or since you're living on land that once belonged to the Amorites maybe you'll worship their gods. I won't! My family and I are going to worship and obey the Lord!

For three minutes, sit still, shut your eyes,
and see what the Lord has for you today.

There are things in this world that are supernatural, good and evil. You have a choice. Who will you serve?

Journal

How do you struggle with free will? _____

_____

_____

_____

_____

_____

In what way does it affect your daily life? _____

_____

_____

_____

_____

_____

Let God guide you. Let go of the reins. Do you feel freedom? How does that feel? _____

_____

_____

_____

_____

_____

_____

God is for us.

He is not against us.

DAY 14: LAST DAY! NEW BEGINNING!

CONCEPT

Jesus saves.

Salvation: We are rescued by Jesus from the power
and effects of sin and eternal death.

Sin deprives us of

ultimate peace	a walk with God
spiritual strength and comfort	seeing and walking in the light
rejecting wicked thoughts	turning away
true love	from temptation
a satisfied life	everlasting life in heaven

PRAYER

*God, I understand You are three in one: Father, Son, and Holy Spirit.
Jesus, today I trust You with my life. I want to give over my free will
to You and trust that my best life is with Your will, not mine. Please
forgive my sins and empower me to stop doing the things in my life that
separate me from You. I ask You to please save me from evil and help me
turn away from and resist temptation. Please take the place in my heart
that is reserved for You, to fill the void, so I can finally feel whole. Today
I ask You to please be my Lord and Savior so I may have everlasting
life. So when I leave this earth, I will live with You forever in heaven.*

We are the sheep. He is our Shepherd. He will protect us from the wolves.

John 3:16 (ESV)

For God so loved the world that he gave his only Son, that whoever believes in him should not perish but have eternal life. For God did not send his Son into the world to condemn the world, but in order that the world might be saved through him.

Psalm 18:30 (ESV)

This God—his way is perfect; the word of the Lord proves true; he is a shield for all those who take refuge in him.

2 Thessalonians 3:3 (ESV)

But the Lord is faithful. He will establish you and guard you against the evil one.

1 Corinthians 1:9 (ESV)

God is faithful, by whom you were called into the fellowship of his Son, Jesus Christ our Lord.

Philippians 4:13 (ESV)

I can do all things through him who strengthens me.

Philippians 4:6–7 (ESV)

Do not be anxious about anything, but in everything by prayer and supplication with thanksgiving let your requests be made known to God. And the peace of God, which surpasses all understanding, will guard your hearts and your minds in Christ Jesus.

For three minutes, sit still, shut your eyes,
and see what the Lord has for you today.

Receive wholeness,

peace, and contentment.

Reject brokenness,

frustration, and anxiety.

CONGRATULATIONS!

Now you have completed the challenge. You have been reborn. Your sins are no longer scarlet but as white as snow. Forgiven and forgotten.

Start fresh, pray often, read the Word, and you will see Jesus come alive in your life.

May God bless you.

He already has!

I pray that this challenge can give hope, peace, and direction to those whose lives deserve more. We have grown accustomed to fear becoming a part of our lives. It is a curse! We cannot move forward if we are frozen in fear. Faith can overcome fear. Faith in God. We need faith in something bigger than government, science, institutions, and society. Unfortunately, humans have too many faults to be pure. Every one of the aforementioned is vulnerable to infiltration of people who are possessed by power, ego, and greed. God wants you just as you are. He will give you peace in the knowledge that He alone is in control. Yes, there is a lot of evil, sadness, and pain in this world. God has given us tough love. He has given us free will. The free will of this world has driven us to where we are today. We live in a world where we are free to accept this gift from God or refuse it. When we lose our faith in God and refuse to live a life pleasing to God, all chaos ensues. That's the world we live in today. No faith, no peace.

Plants need the sun, water, and fertilizer. We need the Son, prayer, and the Word of God.

SO ONE MORE THING

Because of the rule that Satan has over this world, he and his crew are still able to mess with us. We have been saved by the blood of Jesus. He lives in our hearts. He also sends his Holy Spirit to guard our hearts, as we navigate this crazy world in which we live.

By believing and asking Jesus to be our Lord and Savior, we have ammunition against the devil. The name of Jesus gives us authority over Satan and his demons. We don't always realize at first when we are being attacked. It can come as a thought or an idea. It can be a lie that we held onto from the past that the devil keeps bringing to mind. If we nurture it, it will grow and the demon that brought it to you will be delighted. He will rejoice at how easy it was to deceive you. This demon might invite his friends to really give you a problem.

If a thought comes to you and you know it's not godly, reject it! "In the name of Jesus." Use His name and authority to order it away from you. It will leave! That thought will disappear. It won't get a chance to take root and grow. You won't have a chance to act on it. Just snip it out before it has a chance to grow. Every day is a battle for your soul, your emotions, and your mind. But every day you will get stronger in your faith if you read your Bible and pray. Satan hates it! He has no power over Jesus Christ's name or blood.

Your soul is like a garden.

- Praying is the watering.
- Reading the Word is the fertilizer.

You need both to keep your faith strong.

Satan brings the weeds.

Jesus is the cure for

the human condition.

When we are saved, our sins are forgiven. We have no weeds, but we are not sinless forever as with sin the weeds come in. When the weeds blow in, we need to call the master gardener, God the Father, to bring the Son, Jesus, the light of the world. We need to ask for forgiveness every day to keep the weeds at bay.

Ask Jesus to pluck them out at the root every day. The wind could bring a weed, but we can tend the garden with Jesus.

Our journey through life isn't exempt from trials and tribulation. Sometimes things happen that we can't explain. One thing that will never change: you are not alone. The Bible contains answers. Question God, open the Bible, and read it. Sometimes the answer is right in front of you, if you look for it. To gain understanding, we need to study. The Bible can look intimidating and there are many translations. I prefer the Living Bible translation to read and study. It's easy to access and is an easy-to-understand explanation of the books and chapters and their meaning. I highly encourage studying the Bible. It has answers to every situation you could encounter. You can also do a search of a word or topic. You will find answers in the scriptures. A good place to start is the book of John.

I've been praying for a revival. Where people turn away from the evil of this world and put their hope in God. I pray for an awakening in the souls of men and women so they can see the truth. I pray for a revival of the churches of the world and also that people of every color and creed will meet Jesus as their personal Savior. I pray that we can love one another and realize we all bleed the same color and share human DNA. We are the same species, designed and molded by the same Creator. We all sin. No one is perfect.

Sharing is caring.

God told me, "It's time to stop just praying about a revival and that the revival starts with you." Today I sit down with pencil and paper and write what comes to me, "God inspired." If this fourteen-day "Meet Your Maker" Challenge touches you, please help me to start this revival. This teaching can be a spark to start a fire. It starts with one person and grows from here. I pray you have been touched. This is a call to action! It's great to pray for a revival, but now it's time to join and be a part of it. This challenge is an easy way to share your faith and give someone a guide to find God, one-on-one. No awkward conversations or confrontations with family, friends, and others.

Share this challenge with anyone, from family to a homeless person. This will save souls and lives. This will build God's army.

God bless all of us.

Amen.

Drink in the complexities of the Lord. Better than fine wine, He will set your Spirit free.

ABOUT THE AUTHOR

I have been a believer all my life. I didn't truly understand my faith until 1978, about two and a half years before my husband and I married in 1981. In 1983 we bought a house, a business, and a car. We attended church but didn't get involved; we were too busy! We are both hairdressers. We are still working. I am visited by a sea of humanity from my styling chair each day, and my clients share their lives with me. We know each other, not truly. I started thinking that if I were to die, my friends and family would never have known the real me. I'm not brave enough to share my true heart in person so I would have to share my faith and beliefs with friends and family via a letter.

My story is my love letter to you. Holy Heavenly Father gave me this book so I could share with you the real me and what I believe. I've heard so often that people think they have to choose between God and science. Well, I believe that God is the ultimate scientist and mathematician. My Heavenly Father created a world that gives answers, and there are many scientists past and present who could not prove that God does not exist. I've even read that as they made great discoveries many scientists begin believing that there is a Being that started life. I've read that most scientists believe that the theory of evolution can't explain how the one cell organism was created.

I heard that science says that earth is billions of years old. Well, the Bible does not dispute this. The first chapter of the Bible (Genesis) states "In the beginning," which can be billions of years ago. People will say that God doesn't talk about dinosaurs in the Bible. Well, He mentions beasts of the earth. The more I read the Bible, the more I learn that God talks about our earth, it's animals, wars, diseases, pandemics, hatred, violence, and of course people even turning against Him.

I can only tell you that I know and believe in my heart and soul that God does exist. I know that He wants to meet you and tell you who He is. He is the giver of life. He is the almighty, holy, Heavenly Father who loves you unconditionally. He wants to have a relationship with you. He wants you to be able to sit down, without distractions, and share your life with Him. He wants to show you who He is, who He really is, not the God you heard about or inherited.

When someone is famous, we hear all kinds of gossip and innuendo. Rumors about negative aspects of God and His followers have been around forever. But we are all human, and if you measure God by His followers, you will always find fault and failure. We are not perfect. Humans fail all the time. But my God holds true to His promises. He is not the giant flyswatter in the sky just waiting for you to make a mistake so He can take you down. On the contrary, He loves us and wants us to succeed and be joyful and happy. He didn't come to judge us. He came to save us from ourselves and this world we live in.

God's love for us is unconditional. God does not love us based on how good we are, because we could never be good enough to *earn* God's love. But we could never be bad enough to diminish His love. He is here for us *now* as we come to Him as we are.